NIGHT SONG OF
THE PERSONAL SHADOW

GYÖRGY PETRI

NIGHT SONG OF THE PERSONAL SHADOW

SELECTED POEMS

TRANSLATED BY
CLIVE WILMER
& GEORGE GÖMÖRI

BLOODAXE BOOKS

ISBN: 1 85224 107 1

First published 1991 by
Bloodaxe Books Ltd,
P.O. Box 1SN,
Newcastle upon Tyne NE99 1SN.

Bloodaxe Books Ltd acknowledges
the financial assistance of Northern Arts.

Cover reproduction by V & H Reprographics, Newcastle upon Tyne.

Typesetting by Bryan Williamson, Darwen, Lancashire.

Printed in Great Britain by
Bell & Bain Limited, Glasgow, Scotland.

Acknowledgements

The poems in this book are selected from: *Magyarázatok M. Számára* (Explanations for M.), 1971; *Körülirt zuhanás* (Circumscribed Fall), 1974; *Örökhétfő* (Eternal Monday), 1982; and *Azt hiszik...* (What They Think...), 1985. Acknowledgements are due to the editors of the following publications in which some of the translations first appeared: *Child of Europe* (Penguin Books, 1990), *Encounter, Index on Censorship, The Literary Review, London Magazine, New Hungarian Quarterly, Numbers, The Observer, Parnassus, Poetry Review, Poetry World* and the *Times Literary Supplement*. Earlier versions of the introductory essay have appeared in *Encounter* and *Poetry Review*.

Acknowledgements and thanks are also due to the Central & East European Publishing Project for assisting the publication of this book with a grant for the translators.

Contents

Introduction

Hungary is a small nation. Historically, like other small nations, it has often been caught in the crossfire of great powers. Hungarian literature, in consequence, has always been preoccupied with political questions – with history and nationhood and liberty. In this respect, if in no other, the poetry of György Petri is typical. Before the astonishing events of 1989 – which have altered both Hungary and Petri's life almost beyond recognition – to write political poetry was (in his words) 'a moral obligation, because [under Communism] there was no normal canalization for the expression of political opinion'. Though some of the poems in this book are very recent, the time they record is already a past era; the advent of democracy means, for Petri, that he is 'not obliged to participate in political life any more'.

That era may be said to have ended in May 1989 with the removal from power of János Kádár, the pragmatic Communist leader who had ruled the country with Soviet support for more than 32 years. Less than two months later, Kádár was dead. Five months later, the Hungarian Socialist Workers Party was dissolved and the People's Republic declared simply a Republic. Behind all these changes, casting a long shadow over the history of modern Hungary, are the events and personalities of a single month in 1956.

In October of that year, the popular outcry against Soviet domination had overthrown the Stalinist regime and briefly brought to power the now almost mythical figure of Imre Nagy. A Communist of liberal sympathies, Nagy was committed to national independence; he had already been Prime Minister, from 1953 to 1955, but had been expelled from the Party by the Stalinists. The rebellion he now consented to lead was immediately followed by a Soviet invasion and armed resistance by the Hungarian people. By mid-November, the uprising had been crushed; Nagy was arrested by the Russians and subsequently hanged.*

The Soviet invasion brought to power a man as different from his Stalinist predecessors as he was from Nagy. This was János Kádár. Significantly, the prelude to Kádár's eventual demise was the official recognition by the Communist authorities that the events

---

* For a more detailed account of the uprising, see the notes to 'On the 24th Anniversary of the Little October Revolution', 'To Imre Nagy' and 'Cemetery Plot No. 301' on pages 77-79.

of 1956 had constituted a popular uprising. In June 1989, Nagy and his confederates were rehabilitated and, on the anniversary of their execution, solemnly reburied on a national day of mourning. Once this process had been carried out, the collapse of the HSWP and the general election of March 1990 were virtually inevitable. Hungary is now governed by a centre-right coalition that includes a party, the Independent Smallholders, which won the election of 1945, the last time Hungarians went freely to the polls.

Looking back over four decades of Communist rule, it is hard to say which is the more remarkable: the speed of change in 1989 or that things should have changed at all. What ought not to surprise us, however, is the fact that Hungary, long the forcing-ground of political experiment in Eastern Europe, was the first of the Warsaw Pact states to respond to Gorbachev and *perestroika*. Kádár was a paradoxical figure: overtly the creature of Soviet domination and widely regarded as a quisling, yet using his credit with Moscow to liberalise the economy and enlarge the scope of personal freedom in his country. So, in the year of his liberalising New Economic Mechanism – 1968 – Hungarian troops took part in the suppression of the Prague Spring. Moreover, in the early 1970s, when difficulties hit the reformed economy, Kádár rapidly retreated from liberalism.

To a dissident like György Petri, Kádár – 'this Aegisthus, with his trainee-barber's face' – was even more contemptible than the hard-line leaders of other Communist countries. The Hungarian dictatorship, he says, was 'more sophisticated...more clever'; the control it exerted, therefore, went deeper, so 'the moral state of the people' was more dangerously corrupted. As his tone indicates, Petri – despite his taste for flippancy and obscenity – is a rigorous moralist, like all true satirists. He was born in Budapest in 1943, just over a year before the Soviet liberation and five before the Communist takeover. He was 12 at the time of the Soviet invasion and 24 when Czechoslovakia suffered a similar fate. In fact 1956 and 1968 are among a cluster of dates, inescapable in modern Hungary, that punctuate his poems.

For most of Petri's childhood, Hungary suffered under the Stalinist dictatorship of Mátyás Rákosi. From the literary point of view this meant that, for most of the 1950s, such distinguished and largely non-political poets as Sándor Weöres and János Pilinszky were virtually unable to publish. By the time Petri's first books appeared, well into the Kádár era, such restrictions had all but vanished. *Explanations for M.* (1971) and *Circumscribed Fall* (1974) were issued by a state publishing house; yet both would have been unpublishable less than 15 years before, and both contain poems that would still have been banned by most of Hungary's neighbours.

Given such freedoms, Petri's handling of his later collections may seem capricious. In Hungary, official recognition brings a poet prestige and privilege of a kind unknown in the West. But in the early 1980s, Petri turned his back on such success. On submitting a new book to his publisher in 1981, he was informed that thirty of the poems were politically unacceptable, though if they were cut, the book could still be published. He refused. The following year the book, *Eternal Monday*, appeared in *samizdat*.

With *Eternal Monday* Petri had, in effect, exposed the limits of Kádárian liberalism. For most of the 1980s he was excluded from the literary magazines and treated as an unperson in the world of official literature. But what he lost in worldly success he made up for in artistic independence and authenticity of social vision. The evidence is to be found in *Eternal Monday* itself and in its *samizdat* successor, *What They Think...* (1985).

A little before the fall of Kádár, however, all this began to change. Petri's poems began appearing in magazines again and in 1989 a selected poems, *It Exists Somewhere*, was legally published. An unofficial publication, *What They Left Out*, is (as its title suggests) a collection of all the poems not selected – an indication of Petri's innate non-conformity perhaps. Early in 1990 he was awarded the prestigious Attila József prize and a volume of *Collected Poems* is currently scheduled.

Many of the poems published in the 1980s are savage attacks on the political system of the Warsaw Pact as it then was. That being the case, the language is obscene and vituperative, and *samizdat* was the obvious solution to a publishing problem. But it was more than that: it was also in some sense a deliberate choice and, as such, Petri's declaration of independence. This is not to say that Petri now stood alone. In the late 1970s, as the government showed signs of retreating from liberalisation, an unofficial opposition began to appear; but the crucial event that drove Petri and others towards dissidence was the emergence of Solidarity in Poland – and Hungary's decision to ignore it. The satirical squib, 'The Under-Secretary Makes a Statement', written before General Jaruzelski's imposition of martial law in 1981, reveals a profound identification with the Polish cause. During this period, Petri not only demonstrated his support for Solidarity in innumerable ways; he also edited an underground newspaper, helped set up a fund for the families of the unacknowledged poor, signed a public statement in support of Czechoslovakia's Charter 77, and so on.

But there remained a strongly personal element in Petri's dissidence, and this emerges clearly in his poetry. From the outset, ideas of freedom have been central to his concerns. When at the age of 23 he went up to university, it was to study philosophy, and there is a marked philosophical element in the early books. The conception of freedom that runs through both of them smacks of the existentialism then widely fashionable. 'This Square', for instance, strikes me as owing a good deal to Jean-Paul Sartre's phenomenology, the alien otherness of objects compelling the poet to recognise his freedom. And in 'Marriage' we have a Sartrean vignette of emotional inauthenticity, the sexual act becoming for both partners a joyless duty.

Sexuality is often the glass through which Petri discloses the nature of freedom. The same is true of death. As the final limit on freedom, death is evoked by Petri with a morbid physicality and black humour that recall the medieval world. His view of sex is more ambivalent. It focuses the bleakness of the human condition: the temporary nature of our attachments, failures of communication, the mutability of the body, our ultimate loneliness. But it is also an instance and emblem of personal freedom: an activity pursued for its own sake, necessarily private, which no authority has power to control.

Through sexuality, in short, Petri stresses the continuity of the public and private spheres. In 'Gratitude', perhaps the finest of his early poems, the poet (or his persona) wakes to the noises of an enforced public holiday after a night of love-making. His contrast of 'collective idleness' with the intense particularity of the sexual encounter confers on the latter a kind of gratuitous grace to be set against the compulsions of Church or State. Obscenity too has political significance. 'My use of language,' he says, 'was partly a provocation against the unbelievable prudishness of socialist realism and state culture. There's a great silence about sexual life and bodily functions. There's also a sociological prudery, a refusal to talk about the disturbing facts of social or private life.'

In 'Gratitude', Petri's political concerns are heard as noises off, but in the *samizdat* books existential freedom and political freedom are indistinguishable. In the mordantly ironic epigram 'To be Said Over and Over Again', for instance, Petri 'proves' that Hungary is not after all a prison. Kádár's Hungary had all the appearance of a free society, all the trappings: a relatively unmuzzled press, economic enterprise, consumer goods, no obvious restrictions on artistic expression. But these things were there to buy off potential dissent. In reality the country was an open prison. The state granted the individual the right to exist and lead a normal life, but as a privilege that – like an exit visa – could easily be withdrawn.

In the background lies Petri's awareness that the government was itself the beneficiary of such "privileges" – and that in 1956 they had been withdrawn. This preoccupation accounts for the uncharacteristically sober tone of his elegy, 'To Imre Nagy':

> What we can do, though, is remember
> the hurt, reluctant, hesitant man
> who nonetheless soaked up
> anger, delusion
> and a whole nation's blind hope,
>
> when the town woke to gunfire
> that blew it apart.

Petri's attitude to the political class, however, is better represented by the words of his Electra:

> Because of disgust, because it all sticks in my craw,
> revenge has become my dream and my daily bread.
> And this revulsion is stronger than the gods.

As the tone here suggests, Petri is not to be co-opted as pro-Western or anti-Communist or democratic Marxist. This is not to say that he rejects engagement; like many figures from what was the unofficial opposition, he now gives his support to the radically liberal Alliance of Free Democrats, since April 1990 the main opposition party in Hungary. But as a poet his position is essentially and fruitfully negative, which explains why *samizdat* became the *sine qua non* of his poetry's authenticity.

It is Petri's tone, typified by 'Electra', that makes his work so strikingly original. His use of myth and irony will not be unfamiliar to the reader acquainted with, say, modern Polish poetry, but it is hardly typical of Hungarian. Irony is of the essence, and he learned the use of it from foreign poets: from Eliot and Cavafy. The radical tradition of Hungarian poetry, descending from Petőfi and Vörösmarty, the hero-poets of 1848, through the Symbolist Endre Ady, to the modernist and Marxist Attila József, is nationalist, libertarian, Romantic and anything but ironic. Though anxious to suppress the nationalist overtones, the Communists tended to claim this tradition as their own. Thus, its rhetoric of justice and freedom – which Petri finds sympathetic – is no longer available to poetry, as he sees it.

What Petri picked up from Eliot in particular was a mode of

indirection, a means of bypassing such rhetoric, undermining state-imposed obligations and rediscovering the roots of human responsibility in the particulars of relationships. The invention of the staircase, he wittily declares,

> showed wingless man
> the modest trick
> of the detour, when he'd
> try to jump
> in vain after his glance.

He is wary of the ideal and on his guard against verbal inflation of any kind. This may recall other poets from Eastern Europe – Holub and Herbert, for instance, accomplished ironists of the previous generation – but there the similarity ends. Petri is very much of his own generation in his awareness of language as an independent force that can construct reality in its own way. His addiction to word-play, for instance, makes much of his best work untranslatable. Often the full meaning of a poem resides in metalanguage, to be inferred by the reader, because not to be confined within the range of rhetoric the poet is prepared to allow himself. For instance, much of his poetry, like Eliot's, is refracted through the limitations of a pose. The persona seems to owe something to the 'rogue and vagabond' tradition associated with François Villon; he characterises himself as the poet born to be hanged. And yet this self-consciously anti-social stance conceals the severity of a moralist. Petri differs from Herbert or Holub in the peculiarly all-out, unchained quality of his language – whether he broods on the intimate details of sex or verbally flays some swinish secret policeman. In this salutary vigour, Petri is reminiscent of the great satirists of the past – of Juvenal, say, or Jonathan Swift. He is perhaps the outstanding verse satirist of his generation in any European language. As with his progenitors, his bile is the product of injustice and moral outrage.

CLIVE WILMER

FROM **EXPLANATIONS FOR M.**
(1971)

By an Unknown Poet from Eastern Europe, 1955

It's fading,
            like the two flags that, year by year,
we'd put out for public holidays
in the iron sheaths stuck over the gate –
like them the world's looking pale, it's fading now.

Where have they gone, the days of pomp and cheer?

Smothered with dust
in the warmth
of an attic room,
a world dismantled holds its peace.

The march has gone and disappeared.

It metamorphosed into a howl
the wind winnowed.
And now, instead of festive poets here,
the wind will recite into thin air,

it will utter scurrying dust and pulsating heat
above the concrete square.

That our women have been loved seems quite incredible.

Above the era
of taut ropes and white-hot foundries,
the tentative, wary
present – dust settling – hovers.

Above unfinished buildings:
imperial frauds, fantasies.

I no longer believe
what I believed once.
But the fact that I have believed –
that I compel myself
day by day to recall.

And I do not forgive anyone.

Our terrible loneliness
crackles and flakes
like the rust on iron rails in the heat of the sun.

This Square

This square – it's all roar and tremor!
Cars stuck here, their engines running,
the torment of stammering mirrors.

In the stench on a tram platform,
in the dry, late-summer, afternoon heat,
in the chicken-shit's unshakeoffable smell
that pursues from the market-hall

I stand, unsentenced, interned
in a drum savagely beaten.

Incriminating chances beckon:
to choke myself with my tie,
to bite through the wall of a beer-mug: things
parade here, with come-hither poses.

Once I grasp their intent, they leave me
to the risk of my own intention.

And smile from afar.

Winter of 1968

Now that all that mythology's behind you,
you, conscious of your own fallibility,
just sit at home and split your sides

at fatuous old books; you take down
some of the more eccentric treasures
of your library, much as if they were

some potent drink, one closely guarded, saved
for lonely nights – you take small gulps
until it goes to your head and cheers you up.

You go out only to do your shopping;
when a friend comes, you don't sit and chat
but play chess silently late into the night.

Meantime you also work, unhurriedly,
with a lazy diligence.
You write something. Then, for relaxation,

you make scrambled eggs. You have your coffee
sitting by the window,
you put your feet up on the radiator,

light a cigarette, peer out – and feel fine,
even if outside there's a thick fog
rising up the window-pane, opaque, white.

I Loved That Woman Very Much
(to the memory of C.P. Cavafy)

That woman, the heroine of my first
failure in love (my friend's wife),
I loved very much. From the moment we kissed
when the room spun as a matchbox does flipped over
and she slipped gently away, as if swimming.
As she was when I first saw her and fell in love with her
in the swimming-pool, just seventeen years old
(since when, neither I nor my friend have ever
been there again, to that pool, which was where under water
we'd kick ageing actors for bad acting
and would splash, by way of punishment,
one or two cocksure tenors from the Opera)...
Ten years have left on us their...as to what,
let's not be specific. You dress badly.
Since then, you see, I've looked out for such things more.
Or is it perhaps that, aware of
how dress-conscious you are, I notice more?
                        From the moment we kissed
when the room spun as a matchbox does flipped over,
I have sometimes doubted whether I still loved you.
That was two years ago: in the meantime, one way or another,
a lot's happened. Too much perhaps. Can we, can I
look back on those torments with a serious view?

I loved that woman a lot, my friend's wife.
And in 1967 and '68, in cheap cafés
and in my sub-let room on the couch's cynical springs,
with some English books for company, four
dirt-rotten walls, a museum-piece of a typewriter,
and her at thirteen in a supercilious photo,
I knew what it is to be bored.

Air

the world shines
like a dead lizard
or a drop of honey

the world shines
like an old man's hand
or rosewood furniture

the world shines
like the glass
over a picture

'This life of ours bled dry'

This ludicrous life of ours
bled dry
this life verging on shame
De profundis from the depths of a puddle
friendship turning into its opposite
betrayal given a shamelessly instant gloss
the no man's land between disbelief and reason
the nights between a full and an empty bottle
if there is no way to shorten all this
if the hand is too scared to speed an exit
if the stomach is turned by the smell of gas
if affected desire for the bathtub of antiquity
unprincipled hope
cunningly false promises
the nearness the memory of a familiar body
or perhaps sheer curiosity
which is merely the ingrained craving
of the mind for facts
corrupts despair again and again
if our all-too-human belonging
to sleep to waking to the beating of the heart
if the patience of the everyday
weakens the tragic resolve
which allowed to mature would no longer have truck
with the feelings of the average man
who is but the sum of apologetics and anger
a mixture of forward lurching and recoil
if the heating up of the moment
when tomorrow and the next week turn to ash
cannot happen
if over this world of what the eye takes in
the judgement of fire does not flare with a white flame

then the fight
then not even an inch
then backing step by step
no slither of self-deception
never the blur
between silence

and silent acknowledgement
between helplessness and resignation
then our silence
is eyes not turned away
then our presence

and let them decide
what they can do to us

'I am stuck, Lord, on your hook'

I am stuck, Lord, on your hook.
I've been wriggling there, curled up,
for the past twenty-six years,
alluringly, and yet
the line has never gone taut.
It's now clear
there are no fish in your river.
If you still have hopes, Lord, choose
another worm. It's been truly
beautiful,
being among the elect.
All the same, now I'd just like to
dry off, and loaf about in the sun.

FROM CIRCUMSCRIBED FALL

(1974)

Extant Poem by Viturbius Acer

What lies in store for me, for thee?
Do not ask or speak.
In the shade of the fir-shrubs that reappear
scruffily year by year in their wooden tubs,
let us drink up our beer.

Oh knock it back, Leuconoë,
no blank gaping into froth that's ebbed.

Scire nefas – see,
above the caisson of the underground
the grey cement-mixers hum again

– recalling to mind those times –

By the time your blond hair
is dirty with old age,
the streets will have changed. There'll be
a modern frame for the boring, repellent picture.

By spring the new war highway will be ready.
Now like a clattering chariot, January
(whereat, punitive hoar-frost on the trees)
draws near the grovelling provinces.

Now all those who once wanted a future
jerk themselves off into thin air...

Let's withdraw to a table under the awnings –
and another beer!

For hark! the rain thuds down.

To S.V.

The bus was taking me
over the bridge and I looked
on into the tunnel. At
the far end of that pipe
padded with shadows, there were
vehicles hanging about –
quarantined
in an unreachably distant
sandy sun-strip.

A long time since
we were last watching together –
looking out for occasions
to enrich our occasional
poetry with occasions of pain.
Filing away at lyric skeleton-keys
we gauge by sight
for a small circle of friends.

I amble on alone –
the prisoner of a condition it'd be
going too far to call loneliness
and deceiving myself to call independence – on
among parched sights.
I walk down to the embankment looking for shade.
In glass-melting heat
the bus I have just got off
is crawling away somewhere.

An airless tent of chestnuts. But up there
already, the infant stars, as yet
tenderly spiked, herald the autumn.
The water's putrescent slate.
But at least it gets broken up
by a boat putting out from here.
A sight, a view: I've no one
to share it with.
Summer's fruits have ripened
in me and they taste soapy.

I could already tell we were in for a bad year
the morning after New Year's Eve.
In a city of iron shutters, all pulled down,
we slithered about on insidious snow
looking for soak-up soup or hair-of-the-dog.
We ended up drinking iodine-yellow beer
in a surgically tiled café.
And time we stepped outside,
the street was wearing eyesore white.

Our weak brains stop working.
Sailors on ships that are locked in ice,
as is well-known, will devour each other.
Just like the modern Theatre of Provocation –
it all degenerates, banter
into argument, teasing
into insult. Till finally the background
cracks the backbone of the situation.

Now Only

now only the filthy pattering of rain
now only heavy coats and squelching shoes
now only the din of steamed-up cheap cafés
now only trodden sawdust on the stone

now only mouldy buns in cellophane
now streetlights decomposing in thin fog
the advice given by a friendly cop
the last drink bought with the last of the small change

now only the tram-island's desolation
now only the variable course of the night wind
rushing through a town of alleys to no end

now only the unfinished excavations
the night's prospecting-hole its weeds and thorns
now only shivering now only yawns

Message

(Do you remember the German officer
in Vercors's book, the one who had wanted
to conquer France with kindness and Hölderlin –
and then realised his talk was all in vain?)
One day I'll return to you
in the pike-grey of loneliness and power
and you'll know: the food and drink's in vain,
with your flirty hostess jollity you're merely
killing time, your store won't last forever –
it's for your sake that the ring of siege refrains
from crushing the little town: it saves you for me,
so sooner or later you'll steal to my room,
take off your cambric knickers, terrified,
and wring them like some gauche filly of a girl
with her hanky at her first piano exam,
and you go all wet, as if you'd weed in your pants,
worried about your poppet of a husband.
And I, as I know you don't love me,
won't hurry you to open up, oh no,
I'll pet you out of sheer boredom and hatred
as a cat on and off teases a mouse
to make it swoon and its flesh turn all the sweeter.

Stairs

Who was it invented
circumscribed fall
– stairs,
which tame height, the frozen
perpendicular melted
down to degrees; and –
the cunning of the solution –
showed wingless man
the modest trick   .
of the detour, when he'd
try to jump
in vain after his glance?

Gratitude

The idiotic silence of state holidays
is no different
from that of Catholic Sundays.
People in collective idleness
are even more repellent
than they are when purpose has harnessed them.

Today I will not
in my old ungrateful way
let gratuitous love decay in me.
In the vacuum of streets
what helps me to escape
is the memory of your face and thighs,
your warmth,
the fish-death smell of your groin.

You looked for a bathroom in vain.
The bed was uncomfortable
like a roof ridge.
The mattress smelt of insecticide,
the new scent of your body mingling with it.

I woke to a cannonade
(a round number of years ago
something happened). You were still asleep.
Your glasses, your patent leather bag
on the floor, your dress on the window-catch
hung inside out – so practical.

One strap of your black slip
had slithered off.
And a gentle light was wavering
on the downs of your neck, on your collar-bones,
as the cannon went on booming

and on a spring poking through
the armchair's cover
fine dust was trembling.

33

Marriage

Your waist – so often shot through with the pains
of womanhood – pressed back against the stove,
you glance with a joyless peace at him,
this man who's part of the furniture, also a statue.
Your skirt is like a bag of candies, offering
familiar sweetness. Do not resent him thinking
he's grasped what in fact he's misunderstood. (Though already
love's tortuous road has set him panting.)
And it's undesired, the pleasure you combine in
as acid does with metal – eagerly, bleakly.

Lovers

A bee dying on a split
plum's honey flesh.
Together
stewing, rotting,
going gold and black,
in the abandoned garden.

Grace

whoever fate has absent-mindedly
shown favour to becomes quite suddenly
    light amiable and empty
death holds him there poised on a finger-tip
    an eggshell on a water-jet

FROM **ETERNAL MONDAY**
(1982)

Construction

Intellect gushing
over heaps of abandoned fact.

Waking-Dream Image with Maya and Child

The number of your expired identity card
gets pressed into your back,
the courtyard bursts like carbide into flame.
In his sleep the child sits up again, he is dreaming
of his stolen bike and the chief of police
who in silver helmet and Danube Navy uniform
conducts the thief to the scaffold.
In grim pursuit of our pleasure
we row the Styx of dawn.

We hear an old woman's grating voice in the yard,
our sleep treads on bits of decayed rind.
I love you, dear one,
you look at me with burning eyes,
there is brushfire in your glance. Arson
between musty sheets.

Damp walls
sweat out the pain of love,
our fridge boils over.

The margarine is glowing in gold foil.

Dawn
prepares to strike. You can't save me either.
The gas meter keeps clicking. You take a bath. Young children
await you. How can you look at them? I keep
thinking about this. And I don't know...
I am not interested...We settle life
in ourselves, then corpse to corpse we grab each other,
both in a hurry as we fall apart.

Maya

Smooth, dense, homogeneous, saturated:
much like honey. Like a pebble contained
in the round of its own silence.

A "setting state": ice becoming.
Her coefficient of refraction changes a smile's breadth.

And then, of course, getting older;
the varicose veins on her legs,
her swollen ankles.

Apocryphal

The holy family's grinding away –
Mary lies back, God screws;
Joseph, unable to sleep,
starts groping about for booze.
No luck: he gets up. Grabs his things.
Over pyjamas pulls vest and pants.
Then walks down to the Three Kings
for (at last!) a couple of pints...
'God again?'
        'Him again.'
                He sighs,
knocks back his beer, gets wise,
gesticulates:
        'Anyway,
I can tell you, the other day
did I make a fuss: before my very eyes,
the two of 'em on the job!
So I told my Mary straight,
at least shut your gob,
it's enough that the damn bed shakes
and rumbles on as if there was an earthquake.
I mean it now: if he's really got to screw yuh,
I can do without all the ha-ha-ha-hallelujah!'

To Be Said Over and Over Again

I glance down at my shoe and – there's the lace!
This can't be gaol then, can it, in that case.

Song

This is my home,
this is my home,
this is my home: the Wild East
beautiful
Comecon islands
swimming in light.

And the air:
it *is*!
It is just so!
Yes, it *is*! Yes,
it is just so!
(So far.)

The air in our country,
you can drink it in!
In our land you can
drink the air!
Oh this magnificent
air!

Wild East, bewitching East,
there is no getting used to you,
oh you
star-spangled
Comecon islands!

On the 24th Anniversary of the Little October Revolution

Uncle Imre, Uncle Pista and Co
corrected the world's course just a tiny bit.
They were hanged or locked up.
(Uncles Mátyás and Ernő buggered off
to Moscow. And the rest of them shall be nameless.)
Then came the land of Prester John:
'We'll never die!'
The total number of corpses –
and that includes both residents and intruders –
is estimated at somewhere between three thousand
and thirty thousand.
The figure is hard to verify so long
after the event. Many vanished.
Many were made to vanish.
Some people are put on the rack
of forgetlessness.
Some people were put on the rack.
Reality always reckons without herself.
Would she get her sums wrong? Settle her accounts?
A unified and indivisible entity
she failed her eleven-plus
has never properly learnt to count.
I say just two numbers:
56
68.
You can add them, subtract them,
divide or multiply.
Your innumerable doctrines, baseness is their basis,
have failed, are bankrupt.

Night Song of the Personal Shadow

The rain is pissing down,
you scum.
And you, you are asleep
in your nice warm room –
that or stuffing the bird.
Me? Till six in the morning
I rot in the slackening rain.
I must wait for my relief, I've got to wait
till you crawl out of your hole,
get up from beside your old woman.
So the dope can be passed on
as to where you've flown.
You are flying, spreading your wings.
Don't you get into my hands –
I'll pluck you while you're in flight.
This sodding rain
is something I won't forget,
my raincoat swelling
double its normal weight
and the soles of my shoes.
While you
were arsing around
in the warm room.

The time will come
when I feed you to fish in the Danube.

The Under-Secretary Makes a Statement

Four special government committees
and five professors of dialectics with them
have been meeting to study the mysterious
rising-power that is inherent in prices.
The hypothesis put forward by the committees
is that prices have a *randy nature*
and whenever they sight a crowd of housewives
sniffing about in jam-packed queues, they instantly
stiffen like furious Don Juans and rise
and no amount of soothing will bring them down –
entreaties only get them more worked up.
As for wages, they have staying power,
so don't go up, although they do stand fast.
The mysterious working committees have so far –
at a hundred and nine working dinners,
three hundred and thirty-seven working lunches
and two hundred and forty working snacks
(what a job it was to gobble that lot up) –
held discussions in thirty different suites
at a total cost of twenty million zlotys
exclusive of all *per diem* allowances.

But the housewives are impatient –
so many old hags, grannies in particular,
endlessly moaning on about varicose veins
and seeing no further than their carrier bags:
'Meat – meat – meat – meat!' they howl
egging their husbands on to do likewise,
grandpas out on the streets shaking their crutches.
Even the babies wail.

               We simply cannot
work, there's so much noise. So, housewives,
let us, for the last time, make this appeal
to your sober understandings: either you make
your husbands and babies belt up, or else
we cannot be held responsible
and might be driven to perform such deeds
as you would later on regret yourselves.

The key to the situation is in our hands
and we do not shrink from using it to lock up
whole peoples, if that is what necessity dictates.

Autumn

These these these
These hands of shivering children
These beaten
Falling leaves
As they
Keep on snatching grabbing at
Warmth and light and
Fall away rotten before winter
Can make them freeze
These tiny withered hands their gestured pleas

Sweetness

There is no present
I munch at the candied past
Time is a syrup I let it
Congeal into sugar

This Voice in Good Shape Too

While everything is still ahead of us,
it is so good just to look at you,
before deception and disappointment.
This glance
is neither the prelude to anything
nor is it yet a consequence:
it's so good to look at you like this,
without fear, without blame, without accusation.

As if the wind were lightly to stroke a pebble,
as if the water made waves of its own accord,
as if, as if…

But we are not wind or water or pebbles.
We're tender, yes – or is it just weak? – and cruel.
Somehow we'll work out
how to spoil this
as-yet-we-do-not-know-what.

I pity you, lovely creature, you who bring
my cynical body out in goose-pimples –
this comical prospective cadaver,
this candidate for the dissecting-table.
(Not forgetting that, unfortunately,
your future prospects too are much the same.)

O nothing, it's just a woman!
(I say to myself).
And what is a woman?
Hair, skin, mucous membrane.
But why is it so just-there-and-exactly-as-it-should-be?

Dawn: I glance at the castle opposite,
a crumbling Secessionist building
(it's now a computer-stable).
Let there be silence:
the light's fleeting grace redeems
the sin of the bird-fouled plaster ornaments.

Then it all starts over again.

Quatrain

George is the name. I know what I was born for,
Idle away my life, let it go hang.
When they hang *me*, I'll profit by my pain.
Losing my life, I'll win it back again.

Me

God's only-begotten
rotten grape, the one
the old gent keeps for himself
in the frost-freighted garden.

FROM **WHAT THEY THINK . . .**
(1985)

In the Winter of '80

At the close of the mini-epoch
about to begin, I
shall be forty-nine. I've no idea
what will then be in fashion –
what pantie-patterns, what spiritual bric-à-brac.
My young days, by then,
will be long over.
This worm-eaten character,
will he be past (what kinds of) compromise?
What language
will he read the news in?
Will he sleep with the same woman
he's woken beside till now?

Elegy

I could do with having an autumn free of humans
that lasted longer, so I could mull over
the rusting year, picking up on my walk
nuts fallen by the wayside, and the scant yield,
as well, of my "own" hazelnut bushes.
But I won't have one. The customary gloom
of city winters is approaching – that
solemn bailiff with his frosty look.
He takes stock of the autumn's gathered hoard

and, stern though understanding, is astonished
at the lavish squandering this gorgeous lady
has allowed herself. I've been here too
for a while. Explosions, in the sky-deep shafts
of summer, still go on – even here
you can catch the far-off rumbling, the star-mines
of August dynamited.
A walnut thuds on the roof and rolls down
into the gutter. Hoar-frost, rime-frost, snow:
it'll stay up there, that fine brain, and moulder,
as long as this house is ours (though obviously
they may, if they think of it, get the cistern dredged).
On the train you'll be in a bad mood (i.e.
my wife will). Yet again, we're moving house,
back yet again. I, too, am spellbound
by this jostle of wherewithals, by such
a long cortège of cooled-off aspirations:
some Wittgenstein, swimming trunks, a Spanish dictionary,
almond oil – what do we need such paraphernalia for? –
(and that's no more than what I have left up there).
Enough, what we have with us. I'm itching to stay/to go –
like an idiot guest and his over-polite host
pumping each other's hands
in the hall: 'Well, then, then well-then.'
'Till next year then, if we live.'
It's time to go.

In Memoriam: Péter Hajnóczy

1

My simple, singular, old friend is gone:
not to be seen on this restless earth again.
For earth is jealous and will not submit
to sending back one so much part of it.

2

Forgive me for having troubled you.
(As if anyone'd care
a jot for such scruples over there...)
But of those left here so few

phoning me up would find me
so irritable-anxious for their hello:
I'll never meet such another silken buffalo;
though invariably my life is intertwined

with fluffy news, flimsy messages,
logorrhoeic specimens, supernumeraries,
several 'imposing cut-outs', several one-day lays,

and my projects, my pretexts.
Well, rest in peace there: time goes on its way.
That's quite enough rhyming on pain now for one text.

3

I have more and more cravings,
and fewer and fewer days
to tell off to the last one.
By 2030 (a generous estimate)
we shall – with our wives and our enemies,
those who keep eyes on us and those who pant with us –
all of us, all together, all enrich the soil,
the weird deposit bulldozers scoop up out of it.
A child, jubilant, knocks
soil riddled with fine roots out of your eye-socket:
'Dad, can I take this home? Was it a man or a lady?'

4

As regards public-sector cadavers, this year's
crop of corpses has been truly meagre.
The Lionel Longgones and Frank Fuckknowswhos
claim one another, each the other's 'Own Dead'.
Old gourmet of destruction, what a wry face you'd pull
to go through the same self-serchoice menu
for maybe the tenth time.
The populace has been dying
at the usual rate. Those who work, they in the end find bliss.
The latest thing is private mausolea. I find them less and less funny.
You gone, I have taken to browsing
through the deaths column more attentively
and reading the marble ID's they usually have
set up on the resting estates.
The servile soil produces its yews and cypresses,
bells ring, summoning us to follow someone,
on either side of the road there are fat snails
dragging their backs. The priest is about to utter
inanities, the two fat altar boys
fidget like bacon-rind sizzling in the pan.

God gives the sun no cloudy lining,
unmoved he hearkens to his feeble servant,
he beholds the pinky whiteness of women
swaddled in layers of black sweat down to their knickers,
listens to hoarse male singing, sees experts exchanging looks
as they pat into shape the earth-cake decked with flowers. He's trying
to understand something of us. We, dispersing later,
buy savoury nibbles and the Evening News, our ladies'
fine moustaches get sticky with liqueur,
in the tram the widow wobbles, all puffed up –
a busy, white-cuffed paw (her consoler) groping toward her.
We stop off at the (Imitation) Marble Bride and have a few more.
It is all properly done.
I can't tell you much else, Péter. Nothing remarkable
– especially seen from there: through your specks of dust...

Christmas 1956

On the twentieth, at a certain moment
(6.45 a.m.), I, a child of ill omen,
born between Joe S. and Jesus,
become thirteen. It's my last year
of Christmas being a holiday. There's
plenty to eat: the economy of scarcity
was to my Gran as the Red Sea: she crossed over
with dry feet and a turkey. There's a present too –
for me: I control the market still – my one
cousin a mere girl, only four, and I
the last male of the line
(for the time being). Wine-soup, fish, there's everything,
considering we've just come up from the shelter –
where G.F. kept flashing a tommy-gun
with no magazine in it ('Get away, Gabe,' he was told,
'd'you want the Russkies after us?').
Gabe (he won't be hanged till it's lilac-time)
comes in wishing us merry Christmas, there's no
midnight mass because of the curfew;
I concentrate on *Monopoly*, my present –
my aunt got it privately, the toyshops
not having much worth buying. My aunt has come,
in a way, to say goodbye: she's getting
out via Yugoslavia, but at the border (alas)
she'll be left behind, and so (in a dozen years
about) she will have to die of cancer of the spine.
Nobody knows how to play *Monopoly*, so
I start twiddling the knob on our Orion,
our wireless set, and gradually tune in
to London and America, like Mum in '44,
only louder: it's no longer forbidden – yet.
The Christmas-tree decorations, known by heart,
affect me now rather as many years on
a woman will, one loved for many years.
In the morning, barefoot, I'm still to be found
rummaging through the *Monopoly* cards, inhaling
the smell of fir-tree and candles. I bring in
a plateful of brawn from outside, Gran
is already cooking, she squeezes a lemon,

slices bread to my brawn. I crouch on a stool
in pyjamas. There's a smell of sleep and holiday.
Grandad's coughing in what was the servant's room,
his accountant's body, toothpick-thin,
thrown by a fit of it from under the quilt,
Mother's about too, the kitchen is filling up
with family, and it's just as an observer
dropped in the wrong place that I am here:
small, alien and gone cold.

To Imre Nagy

You were impersonal, too, like the other leaders,
bespectacled, sober-suited; your voice lacked
sonority, for you didn't know quite what to say

on the spur of the moment to the gathered multitude. This urgency
was precisely the thing you found strange. I heard you,
old man in pince-nez, and was disappointed,
not yet to know

of the concrete yard where most likely the prosecutor
rattled off the sentence, or
of the rope's rough bruising, the ultimate shame.

Who can say what you might have said
from that balcony? Butchered opportunities
never return. Neither prison nor death
can resharpen the cutting edge of the moment

once it's been chipped. What we can do, though, is remember
the hurt, reluctant, hesitant man
who nonetheless soaked up
anger, delusion
and a whole nation's blind hope,

when the town woke to gunfire
that blew it apart.

If

If the ambitious articled clerk from Simbirsk
had played chess more on Capri with Maxim Gorki
and had listened more to the *Appassionata*,
and, oh yes, if – for he had mused thereon –
he would rather have stroked
than struck,
if he had lost himself in gawping endlessly
at the miracle of Geneva's Central Post Office
(no mind of provincial government could light
upon a thing more admirable), why then...
perhaps there would've been
some trite Kerenskian alternative:
less refrigerstated revolution,
more survivors.

October

Sometimes the dung-fire of hatred will flare up,
sometimes pissed-on slag
starts smoking next to the boiler surreptitiously:
– the dead! the dead! –
Sometimes the people stray-splay out on the streets, rise up,
hold out a chunk of the possible so that it glints
like a stolen earring: not realising it's theirs.
Sometimes, when you've gone, a slight chew of your
                        nipples is what I fancy.

As We Stare Death in the Eye

My unfulfilled loves, scorched up
by this long drawn-out autumn,
are turned voracious old women.
These bits of overripe cheese
are lying about ungrated.
Yet a spitting distance away
is the other world.

Theosophy
(for Aliz)

If there *is* a God,
he's a general of peasant birth.
His star-spangled uniform
our goal, we are led astray
further and further from home –
into snow and howling *taiga*.
Ahead of us on the frost
he keeps shimmering: he is
a Kutuzov with no Moscow.

Electra

What *they* think is it's the twists and turns of politics
that keep me ticking; they think it's Mycenae's fate.
Take my little sister, cute sensitive Chrysosthemis –
to me the poor thing attributes a surfeit of moral passion,
believing I'm unable to get over
the issue of our father's twisted death.
What do I care for that gross geyser of spunk
who murdered his own daughter! The steps into the bath
were slippery with soap – and the axe's edge too sharp.
But that this Aegisthus, with his trainee-barber's face,
should swagger about and hold sway in this wretched town,
and that our mother, like a venerably double-chinned old whore,
should dally with him simpering – everybody pretending
not to see, not to know anything. Even the Sun
glitters above, like a lie forged of pure gold,
the false coin of the gods!
Well, that's why! That's why! Because of disgust, because it all sticks
     in my craw,
revenge has become my dream and my daily bread.
And this revulsion is stronger than the gods.
I already see how mould is creeping across Mycenae,
which is the mould of madness and destruction.

RECENT POEMS

Cold Peace

In the absence of peace, your plain man's mind might think:
there will be war. There being no war,
your learnèd mind would believe:
this now is peace. But it is and will be neither.

[1987]

Morning Coffee

I like the cold rooms of autumn, sitting
early in the morning at an open window,
or on the roof, dressing-gown drawn close,
the valley and the morning coffee glowing –
this cooling, that warming.

Red and yellow multiply, but the green
wanes, and into the mud the leaves
fall – fall in heaps,
the devalued currency of summer:
so much of it! so worthless!

Gradually the sky's
downy grey turns blue, the slight
chill dies down. The tide
of day comes rolling in –
in waves, gigantic, patient, barrelling.

I can start to carry on. I give myself up
to an impersonal imperative.

[1986]

Sisyphus Steps Back

The age of intrepid idiots is upon us.
Fools or knaves? They're both at the same time.
I'm scared of understanding, and yet I laugh at it:
you can't stop a boulder once it's rolling back.

[1988]

Cemetery Plot No.301

Let everything stay as it is!
With the carcasses from the Zoo?
Why, yes. Was their fate any different?
Was hanging any kinder than putting to sleep?
I cannot forget (when I say this,
I don't mean to threaten: it's the way I am:
I'm not able to forget).

On the other hand, what would I wish
for myself if I'd been – ha-ha! – hanged?
if I were to come back as a Stone Guest?
I'd wish at long last to be left in peace.
I shit on reverence. To these men
more mercy should've been shown when they were alive
(they should've been left alive). Now it's too late.

Against death there is no *remedium*.
No compensation for widows,
orphans, nations. I'm not interested
in the hangman's mate and his belated tears.
My eyes are dry. I need them for looking with.

Though actually there isn't much
to see – only, in the dusk
everything gets sharper:
a female body, a branch,
the downs of your face. I don't want
anything. Just to keep looking, no more.

[1989]

72

Notes

16-17. **By an Unknown Poet from Eastern Europe, 1955:** The date is significant. Petri is thinking back to the darkest days of Mátyás Rákosi's Stalinist regime, just before the uprising of 1956.

19. **Winter of 1968:** i.e. just after the Warsaw Pact invasion of Czechoslovakia.

27. **Extant Poem by Viturbius Acer:** The poem alludes to Horace's *Ode* I, xi, which includes the famous injunction *Carpe Diem* ('Seize the day'). The ode begins 'Ask not, Leuconoë – we cannot know – what end the gods have set for me, for thee'; 'we cannot know' translates the Latin, *scire nefas*. Reference is also made to the construction of the Budapest metro, begun in the early fifties but soon abandoned for lack of funds. It was eventually completed in the early sixties.

28-29. **To S.V:** Addressed to Petri's friend and fellow poet, Szabolcs Várady. The opening stanza refers to the spectacular Adam Clark suspension bridge, which spans the Danube in the centre of Budapest. On the mountainous Buda side, the road over the bridge leads directly into a tunnel, the far end of which is visible from the bridge.

31. **Message:** Vercors: French novelist of Hungarian origin, active in the *Maquis* during the Second World War.

33. **Gratitude:** The public holiday in this poem is probably the anniversary of the Soviet liberation of Hungary, 4 April 1945. This used to be celebrated every year with a salute of guns.

44. **On the 24th Anniversary of the Little October Revolution:** 'Uncle Imre': Imre Nagy, Hungarian Communist leader. Minister responsible for major land reform, 1945. Prime Minister from 1953 till 1955, when he was expelled from the Party. Prime Minister of revolutionary government, October–November 1956. Hanged, 1958.

'Uncle Pista': István Bibó, political scientist and key theoretician of reform movement. Member of Nagy's cabinet, 1956. Sentenced to life imprisonment, 1957, but released after amnesty, 1963.

'Uncles Mátyás and Ernő: Mátyás Rákosi and Ernő Gerő, Stalinist leaders. Rákosi fell from power in July 1956 and was removed by the Russians to Moscow. He was succeeded by Gerő, who fled to Moscow during the uprising.

45. **Night Song of the Personal Shadow:** During the period of his political activities, Petri was subjected to surveillance by the security police.

The end of the poem is probably meant to evoke the last months of the Second World War in Budapest. At that time, the Hungarian Fascist movement, the Arrow Cross, executed Jews and deserters by lining them up on the embankments of the Danube and shooting them into the river.

46-47. **The Under-Secretary Makes a Statement:** Ironic comment on the recent history of Poland, written between August 1980 and December 1981, shortly after the emergence of Solidarity but before the imposition of martial law.

50. **This Voice in Good Shape Too:** The Secessionist movement in architecture and design was the Austro-Hungarian equivalent of *Art Nouveau*. There are many large Secessionist buildings in Budapest, which date from the turn of the century.

57-58. **In Memoriam: Péter Hajnóczy:** Hajnóczy (1942-81) was a Hungarian writer noted for his experimental prose (e.g. the short novel, *Death Rides Out from Persia*, 1979).

'Each other's "Own Dead"': Petri here parodies a formula used in official announcements of death – e.g. 'The Party regards X as its own dead and takes responsibility for the funeral expenses...'

59. **Christmas 1956:** i.e. two months after the uprising. 'Between Joe S. and Jesus': Stalin was born in December too. *Monopoly*: in Hungary the game was called *Capitaly*.

61. **To Imre Nagy:** The poem deals with the events of 23-24 October 1956 and the execution of Nagy in 1958. On the evening of the 23rd, a crowd of about 100,000 assembled outside the Parliament building in Budapest to demonstrate against Soviet domination and for democracy. They called for Nagy to take over the government. In an unsuccessful attempt to calm them down, Nagy spoke extempore from the balcony. Still outside the government, he was appointed Prime Minister during the night in response to the acclaim. Fighting began in the early hours of the following morning when Soviet troops entered the city. In November, when the uprising had been suppressed, Nagy was arrested and deported to Romania. In June 1958 he and four other Ministers were tried *in camera* and hanged in a prison yard on the outskirts of Budapest.

62. **If:** The title is in English. 'The ambitious articled clerk': i.e. Lenin. The poem alludes to various incidents in Lenin's life and, in particular, to his occasional remarks on matters of culture. He was fond of Beethoven's *Appassionata* sonata; and he once remarked that he wished he could have achieved his ends by 'stroking' people instead of fighting them.

65. **Theosophy:** Kutuzov: Russian general in the 1812 campaign. His strategy of evasion was largely responsible for the destruction of Napoleon's forces.

72. **Cemetery Plot No.301:** When Nagy and his colleagues were hanged, their bodies were immediately dumped in a cemetery adjacent to the prison. Their grave, unmarked, was plot no.301. In June 1989, on the 31st anniversary of their deaths, the bodies were exhumed, coffined, given the full honours of a state funeral and reburied in plot no.301, now suitably memorialised. It was found, when the graves were first opened, that the bones of animals from a nearby zoo had been buried along with them.